Cleveland Poets Series No. 53

Willow from the Willow

Margaret H. Young

Cleveland State University Poetry Center

Acknowledgments

These poems originally appeared in the following:

"What the Pictures Say," *Zuzu's Petals Quarterly*, 1993
"Christmas Colors, Rochester, New York" *The Baffler* #6, 1995
"Transit," *Medela Review* #1
"Stopping in San Francisco on the Day Before Thanksgiving,"
    Thumbscrew, #3 1995
"Walking Around Meadville, PA," *Brass City* #1, 1996
"Mole Ghazal," *Poetry Motel*, 1996
"Vow" and "Liner Notes for a Mix Tape," *Mockingbird*, 1996
"Landscape with Reservoir and Extended Family" and "How I Will
    Explain," *The Heartlands Today* #6
"Thanks to Persephone," *Half Tones to Jubilee*, 1997
"A Door of Bees" and "Crinoline Nocturne," *The Oil City Review*, 1997
"Students of Ripeness," *The Oil City Review*, 1998
"Cough," *The Café Review*, 1998
"Willow from the Willow," *Antietam Review*, 1999
"The Black Dog," Festival of Voices anthology, CCAC Allegheny
    Campus, 1999
"What We Feel" and "Stochastic Resonance," *The Exchange*, 1999
"Extras," *Crazyhorse*, 1999
"Video Screenplay," *Mississippi Review*, 1999
"Light Bulb," *Arts and Letters*, 2000

Published by Cleveland State University Poetry Center
1983 East 24th Street
Cleveland, OH 44115-2440
ISBN: 1-880834-54-5

Library of Congress Catalog
Card Number: 2001097849

The Ohio Arts Council helped fund this program with state tax dollars to encourage economic growth, educational excellence and cultural enrichment for all Ohioans.

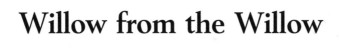

Willow from the Willow

Contents

"For my mother and father"

Rituals, Day of the Dead

We don't scatter marigold petals here,
hold picnics in the graveyard, not on this cloth
of ginkgo fruit and leaves.
We should anoint ourselves with stench
like these dogs we walk, shoulder some rot.

You jump from sleep into the air of Thursday
and your mother is not there to catch you
again, her face not smiling
from the promised first snow clouds, her voice
not at your houndstooth sleeve
saying forward, forward,
eat this bread, forgetting me,
lick the sweet white ice of tomorrow.

Mole

Start with garlic, onions softened
in hot oil, some alchemy you've smelt before.

Open the wine early, a six dollar bottle, red as curtains:
let half of it drink into sauce.

Get three kinds of chilies, whisper their glistening names:
ancho, poblano, serrano, crumpled like slippers, lean as racehorses.

The right hand holds almonds, the left sesame.
Seeds toast apart but grind together, hot and damp.

It looks wrong until you fold
in chocolate: one square, melting slowly,
two, the corners disappearing, then three makes it dark enough.

To reconcile salt, sugar, pepper, acid:
keep tasting until lips and tongue say yes.

Looking for an Animal Totem

1. Santa Cruz

These sea lions—slung on beams like overfed barn cats
   or eddying darkly, cow eyes gleaming—
   groan and belch at us, up here
   with our cameras and longings and paper sacks of fudge.
Why *do* we stare so fondly?

Seven years ago, up to my neck
   in equator-water with two huge pups,
   all slow and elbows to their sleek plunging,
I thought, this *must* be play, dancing to them, too—

Walking back to sand between surf shops,
postered maps of the bay
I hear another sea lion out there?
A swirl, a head—an otter!
   supple, crunching a shell between its paws,
   twisting and lolling between air and water,
   just close enough to hear me call.

2. Davis

For olives, these three
(two male, one female mallard)

brave the curb and bike path to this lawn:
they beak obsidian fruit and nod it down
with the delicate greed of students at a catering tray.
The smell here's oil, imported sun-white stone
under steely leaves and windows

but these ducks could have stepped
from Plum Creek in Ohio—
their toy-shape, mutter, wag and walk
homey as sugar maple, trout lily, cardinal call.

3. Pt. Reyes

No whales today.
We pull up to the continent's edge
    and scatter down a dune.
Two lines of geese across the clouds' gray
    screens light toward another sunset.

I step to sand licked dark four waves ago,
    stare at the folding hem of foam.
The next wave rises sudden, full,
    swirls over knees
    to smack between my thighs,
    wetting my lifted dress and underwear.

Stalk

Burst bud casings litter the ground;
nuts thrust a pale toe earthwards.

Fiddleheads unfurl, stiff curves crusted with scales,
future fronds beckon from last year's dead.

Jack's pinstripe pulpit still limp and wrinkled:
he's in there kneeling, praying for us all.

Knotweed has this hollow snap, red tip,
slimes the fingers, cooks down olive green.

Download the fractals. Watch May etch and bloom,
watch dripping leaves unroll across the screen.

Light Bulb

You can see where the white part joins
the leaf, there's some red there
between: that's blood, flowing
from rock to air, connecting them.
It breaks off only
stubbornly, clinging
riverbottom dirt
crumbly as cheap Easter chocolate, eggs and ears
of soil in roots. You can see the red umbilical
and a hood of slimy gray, speckled with darkness:
the caul, that giving up
to breathing. And so the moon
bleeds its birth, night leaf
pulling water, light from behind,
white root swelling from slit
to slip
to drop
to cup
to glowing whole in the sky.

Crinoline Nocturne

Cats stare blank as children,
perched on shrouded cars.
Four sprinkled blocks east,
a marching band throbs,

the crowd sighing.
Rhinestone eyes
of fish on my skirt
stare back. Between streetlamps

light from stars, lit panes
of hollow bungalows.
Starched willow ribbons
hang a rustling sidewalk curtain.

Downtown, a siren howls
but velvet driveway roses
—red even by sodium glare—
hold themselves poised, unruffled.

A Door of Bees

Rococo cumulus keep switching the light:
in sun the beige back stoop
where milk was once delivered to the mansion
now hums golden, alive as bees thread
insistent flowerless tracks above the mat,
along the screen, wanting in or out like cats.

Drinking strawberries in March might be the problem.
In this valley the season is far gone,
petals in gutters already pulp,
colors more of another equinox:
schoolbus yellows of poppies and ripe fruit,
iris and lupine dark as ironweed.
And calla lilies rise from bungalow beds—
we're all transplants, blinking, mixed;
learning these steps can take a while.

The Hearts

I saw them once, at Conneaut Lake Park,
September, one of those vamped oldies clubs
with half a pink car hanging on the wall.

"He never takes me dancing," said the doctor's
wife, explaining why we might be asked along,
born seven years after the Hearts' last hit.

We should just hire ourselves out, we joked:
the Steves to jitterbug, flirting and safe;
Mark with his litany of hits and years,
Charlotte and I in vintage taffeta.
Our season finished, small-town winter looming:
we just wanted a roof, a stage, a beer.

We watched Lee Andrews, tried to calculate
his age: the other Hearts were all his family
now, three skinny sons on drums, keyboards,
bass, plus matching wife and daughter dressed
in matching slinky fuchsia singing back-up.
Jeri curls gleaming, more than well-preserved,
he played us like a preacher, lithe and proud.

The other big group at the gig that night
was a reunion, this extended family
in matching t-shirts printed with their name,
the date, labeled like jars of homemade jam
or marathon runners, a whole funeral's worth
of generations gathered for this dance,
tables of red, laughter, and back-slapping;
they formed a conga line, surrounding us.

Stepping outside for cool air on my arms

I leaned on rails over the rustling water,
pulled rhinestones from my aching ears,
suddenly remembering to be lonely.

A girl in a red t-shirt, Down Syndrome,
came from the noise and joined me on the porch.
She looked out at reflected lights from boats,
the crumbling inn, the satin sky, and said
"It's *mantic*," grinning, her blunt face shiny
with sweat.   Inside the Hearts were on break
while the DJ spun some song we'd heard
too many times to care; they all danced on.
But I grinned back and said
                              yeah sister, it is.

Seasoning the Pot

I lay them on the rug:
(our home so young it's tableless)
the tea things, pot cooling.

Before the leaves
a splash of water
inside, then poured out.

A simple ritual or trick
passed on in other kitchens,
earlier afternoons.

This pot, like our cups and kettle
worn smooth as beach pebbles,
unmatched, familiar.

The cracks inside are stained
browner with each brewing,
a finer print than tea leaves.

Cough

Small beast in my chest all week, dry paws
grasping trachea, furred tail
curved through the smaller tubes. I feed it
sweet liquid from brown bottles and it sighs,
folds up and sleeps a while.

I can hear it breathing behind me,
one beat late. When it wakes
it wants to talk and won't take no.
I bow gently, cup my hands
to hear. Its voice is thick, salty and old.
It says one word over and over
in a language I've forgotten, leaving a taste
of gray stone on my tongue.

Housesitting: Variations

1. Fingers, June 1996

Fresh coat of Wet 'n' Wild Strong Nail
went on stringy, blotched, an old batch
scrabbled from cabinets no longer mine;
backs scratched from berry brambles
or cat mad at being kept from killing
(where's that baby now, storm water
gunning from the eaves, it didn't want
my worms, no sucker for my cheeping,
I'm no mother); rose-dirt, leash-burn—
this one wears her ring, carnelian;
this one wore her mother's diamond last time
I was married in a play and who knows,
might again

2. What the cat dragged in

is a baby robin squat as a clod,
pin feathers sticking out like old men's hair.
I save it because I am queen of the universe,
able to lift pliant sharp-toed cats from plundering,
to bend calmly to young basil amid cardinal arias,
to bike past fat naked houses
newly-built on good farmland and not weep
because change crawls cheerful as the smell of wounded grass
where Tom Saxbe is mowing down by Plum Creek,
where the baby robin lies now after all,
only the latest in a series of failed interventions
while the wedding dress still zipped in brown vinyl

hangs next door teaching patience
in a closet full of gaps as the horizon
where a dozen white pines
joined up last spring's storm:
through those new holes
dead stars shine on, money for nothing.

3. Half-assed dog walk through downtown Oberlin, Ohio

Thunderstorm came knuckling in,
stuck me and hound on co-op porch on College Street
across from some undeterred folk charring beef
and blasting Mix 93, Shake That Thing
while heaven shakes its thing.
So counting intervals and waiting for a break
of course this little girl in turquoise shirt
and rubber barn boots comes along and grins at me,
(prissy dry 30, responsible
with disks, clean sneakers to protect)
and proceeds to the swing where she proceeds to swing
a little token bit but mostly dips up mud
and smears it over herself until black stretch pants,
boots, t-shirt and arms are gloriously wet gray brown
and she is smiling not just at me now as if to say
to the whole world perhaps, what's your excuse?

How I Will Explain

I'll talk about the weather: postcard June,
then record hot then jacket cool with storms
before the solstice dawn or looming
through an afternoon, crackling the radio—
they'd tell us after the monotone howl to "stay
calm but alert to rapidly changing conditions."

So I tried that: calm but alert. I stood
in rain, in the knee-deep street,
watching the flow wash
leaves and take-out lids to French Creek,
Riviere aux Boeufs, In-un-ge-ch, water
that's had its name and flow change, river
to lake and back, three times since the last ice age.

In Blooming Valley the tornado peeled off roofs,
shoved trees into barns. I drove
past the wreckage, families picnicking,
to pull tall weeds from beetle-sequined kale,
bolted spinach and arugula,
late tomatoes I'd given up on.

I'll talk about how swallow fledglings learn:
by flying badly, bumping into things
for days. How one sat on the barn floor
barely moving, a clump of manure-colored
feathers, small hunched head
facing the door
where the parents soared easily
against the clear midsummer sky.

Stopping in San Francisco on the Day Before
Thanksgiving

I sit on the lowest step of a pyramid made of the same color
    granite I picked to mark my mother's grave,
rose speckled with black and gray in three darknesses,
among concrete urns overflowing with gauche, long-stemmed
    impatiens.
Around me move plump clean-shaven men with flowered
    neckties and stiff briefcases,
soft men in sweaters walking slowly, their white hair falling
    into their eyes;
young women in threes clutch wallets and laugh,
thin polished women hurry in raincoats and flat shoes:
heading back to carpeted offices after lunch,
pausing to light cigarettes and look up at the narrow sky,
talking with expressive hands at white plastic cafe tables.

Pigeons also go about their business on the pink granite floor
    of the plaza,
pacing, their plump throats throbbing at every step.
Some wear more mineral green and violet on their necks,
some have stuck-up whitish feathers rumpled as if from a
    clothes dryer,
but they all wear the gray uniforms of pigeons in London,
    Manhattan, New Haven,
the birds of cathedrals, quadrangles, fountains and war
    memorials.

I am also dressed in gray this afternoon:
my mother's Paris wool, Ann Arbor thrift store pleats, a coat a
    student left at my father's house,
a scarf cross-striped in two shades of gray silk from the
    Chicago grandmother I have no memory of;

pieces of travelers and destinations far away, yet with me now
as I watch here in the hours between buses in and out of San
    Francisco,
clothed in the gray of the November sky charged with thin
    sunlight,
gray of cigarette ashes falling from the white plastic cafe tables,
gray as the crystal flecks of granite shining throughout this
    downtown plaza
where pigeons bow politely to gifts of crumbs.

Students of Ripeness

In my California house
we get fruit from the lab black
marker-inked with data,
mostly hard and green;
but this week there came
four pineapples in three
days so ripe they filled
the kitchen with sugar-smell;
their armadillo skin
was flattened, coppery; and their flavor
had a caramel smoothness, a depth
and essence of the fruit you can't
buy on this continent;
you have to live with students
of ripeness.
         My housemate wields
a knife and slice of yellow
dripping skin, homesick
for Costa Rica—*This*
is pineapple, he breathes, and suddenly
I understand foreignness,
how he can buy apples
waxy and swollen from the supermarket,
those perfect red and yellow
flavorless Delicious—this student
of ripening itself is versed
in honeydew, laughs at what pass
for plantains here, but hasn't
driven seven miles through spent
cornfields expressly for an apple,
or two bags of them, two
flavors chosen from six

or more: heart-, biscuit-,
or globe-shaped, striped, blushing,
or dappled Cortland, Pippin,
Macintosh or Jonagold.

Or ridden a borrowed bike
four miles over
and over to a house you've helped
empty all week of forty
years of magazines,
hotel soaps and stationery,
taking cigarette holders,
hats, and photographs of you,
that look like you, that don't—
because even the trees are full there.
You should be working; you've spent
too much time gathering
already, but one thing
you've carried from that house is a lesson
about ripeness: these apples
are nameless, mildew-etched, worm-
bored, scarred and puckered,
falling to mash and bee-haze
underfoot, but they taste crisp
and complicated, you think of wine,
the ocean, red-tiled
floors burnished with passage,
silk scarves folded
in drawers. So you fill
grocery bags, your backpack,
bike basket; wobbling
across town you want

to toss them to freshmen saying
here, eat this, don't
ask why; you fill the cleaning
lady's arms, copper
bowls, crusts; your sister's
head with pastry rules,

giving in to this mood—
not heartbreak, blues
but yellows, reds, old
summer greens and browns, baking
these hard late fruits.

Willow from the Willow

Learn about pines from the pine,
and bamboo from the bamboo.
                    —Basho

Sad Michaelmas under a weeping sapling,
little *Salix* with no river to cry leaves into,
just this brick half-circle fountain,
plaster Mary holding broken hands
out to us.

Why weep, so green and yielding in the wind?
You thrive on light of cornered stones,
send roots between these buildings, learn
to bend to breeze-flux, water-pull;
holding on to leaves in autumn last and last
to fold them out in spring.

Look up over rooftops at blue buttermilky
Michaelmas sky: there floats a feather,
white, pigeon probably
and timed like the best joke,
spinning on that late September wind,
falling and rising in the air
that stirs green willow branches,
talks back to the fountain
where Mary blesses bricks and perfect platters
of nasturtium leaves and nightshade
with its wound-red berries.

On Michaelmas it's good
to drink dark drinks from flame blue mugs
and pick black walnuts, green and soft
as olives, dry as aging hands:
smell their sour flesh, know
there's so much left to learn.

At the Beehive Coffeehouse

Sometimes you get it sitting behind glass
between two spiky trees in pots, watching a cop
poised rocking on his silver bike.
His black and yellow jacket says he's Ferelli.
Glenn Miller's "Skylark" playing,
down at the river, seagulls and ducks
had nothing to say to me.
I'd like to Supergirl these roofs,
dark patches, pass the cars from high.

A book by the cash register
"published with help from Corporate Media"
explains how the poet has found God.
I've found a coalblack dog to walk
two times a week, a poem about bees.
I've found the movie that I live in
isn't that original. Sky gray-bright,
the barely detectable eclipse done
so we're back to an ordinary afternoon
towards the end of something.
Rabbits by the construction site
nest among blocks of concrete. Tossed
cigarette butts catch light in the street;
bees of the invisible fly in and out
unnoticed as sparrows.
Two sisters in yellow hats and gray down coats
hobble tandem down East Carson Street.
A priest blessed the river: dropped cross
tied to a string. The news
predicts more storms.
These wounds will heal.

Looking for Place in All the Wrong Loves

But the yellow—you turn your head:
Hope lasts a long time if you're happy.
　　　　　—William Stafford, "Yellow Cars"

The day you see the pierogi car off East
Carson on Twentieth it's parked,
promoting Mrs. T's Mini Pasta Pockets
by a tent shading two butter-slick
steam tables. Used to live near Shenandoah
(PA, home of Mrs. T's),
you tell the aproned woman spooning
small pierogis into paper boats,
pronounce it Shendo,
as the coal town's natives do,
to rhyme with zendo.
The car is bright yellow,
brand new Volkswagen;
painted cartoon pierogis
bloom over its curves,
half moons, wings of yellow ladybugs.
You take the plastic fork,
serving of promotional Cheddar
Jalapeño and Potato Cheese,
through July sunbeat on asphalt
through the street fair,
dearth of shade trees here,
you have to go down to the river
to sit by sycamores.
Listen to some jazz,
eat warm pasta pockets,
go down to the river,
walk streets clogged with summer and regret,

you go down to the river, you report
as arranged at the Information Booth,
you go down to the river, hear it
before you see it, motorboat wake
slapping the shore,
you go down to the river,
left this bank last winter,
you have wept among these mulberries,
walked the black dog here,
you go down to the river,
sit on the moss- and liverwort-stitched bank
and put your feet nearly in water,
you go down to the river,
touch wet pebble, clamshell,
smell the water flowing to Ohio.

O.K. to Rip Off Joseph Cornell

because these things, in fading, never fade:
        green parrots profiled on varnished blocks
        brass bees flying in formation
        three wooden spheres asleep in their sockets
        the bottle dreaming the feather
        the pin dreaming the butterfly wing.

Meadville Diary

1. Council on the Arts

Class meets in the theater across
from the gallery and studios where
Jackson Five blares over thumping feet
next door to black-robed gentlemen
who push tigers and monkeys through thick walls.

Take two steps forward and a photograph
the bulletin board coughed off five years ago:
you wearing white to play another fool.

Red brick, gray stone braid wind
into component voices. Blues sung
by doves and old men now.

2. South Main at Mill Run

Worm-smell rises from the wet road,
clouds wrap the day.

Back up the river after onions, ears:
hope for a rising,

for the foolishness of trout. Still waters
run in my sleep.

3. Strawberry Season

Cold fire on Tamarack Lake,
full moonscape, cloud-framed.

Wright of Derby

visits America, gets drunk with Thomas Cole.

Together they smell a valley that
one hundred years will fill with spring-flow, stream-run,
hold crayfish, canoes and yearnings,

drip with moon-breath, reflect
sky-milk
         and meteors,
satellites and sighs.

4. Recurring Theme

Stars drown in puddles of a town
so old, leaving takes light years.

Sweep me down, three feet's enough,
gamble my equilibrium and lose.

Time drips, sap from cut twigs.
Everybody's walking on thin clouds.

In Becky's kitchen, late September,
three squat peppers, red and sweet,

rest on their knuckles in
the glow of afternoon.

Christmas Colors, Rochester, New York

1.

Driving in circles:
the same strip where
three neon bagels
stare across a traffic signal:

another sign, lit red
optician's spectacles
starts us on *Gatsby* jokes,
remembering high school symbolism,

the colors saying
danger or *rebirth*.

2.

The kids found a loophole
on the ban on gang colors
in school: Santa hats.

3.

The squirrel nibbles a candy cane
in the park's printed snow,

holds it upright
(clarinet, microphone?)

then sideways
(flute, corncob?)
then runs it up an evergreen
away from our laughing.

4.

Roommates menstruating at the same time
is known as the McClintock effect.

No name for this: my brother's roommates
appear one breakfast,
all four in red sweaters.

5.

Sugar fluoresces, wintergreen snaps
ultraviolet light when struck or bitten.
Atomic Fireballs burn cinnamon, then roll
slowly to sweetness, staining our tongues.

6.

A papier mâché fly circles the bar,
green bulb eyes glowing.
We drink from green bottles
under a green ceiling dragon,
dance below a replicated 50's livingroom
tired of waiting for a good song.

The mirrored ball spins out
red rings of light, a galaxy of platelets played
across our limbs, the upside down Formica chairs.
Outside the gift of rain is general,
weighing down the branches
of put-out Christmas trees,
helping rot apples and Osage oranges in Ohio,
soaking the parsley in my California garden,
dissolving last year's snow like sugar,
thawing us like an unexpected kiss.

Stochastic Resonance

According to the thrift store
today the universe is saying *plaid*:
bright colors brightest next to black,
the blunt yes of the perpendicular.

Best soup this season:
bag of last-leg vegetable scraps,
jar of nearly moldy tomato sauce,
five wilted beet tops,
and blessed garlic, holy onion.

Cardboard, glass and wire
to back the mother
young in grainy black-and-white
on the beach, the lake
before it died:
her whole body twisted to the moment
just after throwing a stone into the waves,
dark hair and clothing loose, wind-tossed,
face north, away from lens
to water, to horizon.

A tap dance class, late afternoon
sunlight streaming in, eighty metal keys
on golden boards nearly together,
together.

Cut: not the lemon but the fingertip.
Sugar to clot, bandage
catching on glove for weeks, pain of typing
f, g, t, r, b, v, body
insisting here, here, here.

Lenses: fog and break. Replacement
vision in the mother's chunky period frames.

Love: plunged in and out in weeks,
heart snaps elastic, asks for more.

The ten year anniversary of the mother's death:
spent taping sentimental songs, falling
down sled-packed slopes.

What the Pictures Say

We lived familiar with our beauty.

Sometimes we dressed deliberately, posed—
    lifting sherry, in evening gowns on living room floors;
    or hair down, blurred, nothing but strung coins covering breasts—

but mostly we just looked like that:
    standing before a barn in France or Ohio,
    hands in jacket pockets, smiling sideways;
    or crouched on brick museum steps with cigarettes;
    holding smooth white knees and elbows at the beach.

There were men sometimes, of course:
    leaning on deck rails, windy-haired;
    bending to maps at cafe tables,
    heads back on plaid blankets in grass—

but they were more part of the reasons not to marry,
    like curly dogs in the front seats
    of big-fendered cars we picked out ourselves;
    reading in wide calm chairs by the lake;
    desks where our hands moved among slides and cardfiles,
    absorbed, looking up only to smile quickly, assured
    at each other, at ourselves.

Thanks to Persephone

Snapshot of her on a bridge in Paris:
black jacket with wide curved lapels,
hair helped back by a silver clip,
she shields a cigarette from the wind
        in nineteen fifty-one.

I can go all day unthinking now;
then her old earrings press my lobes,
a bad movie shows a hospital room,
or there's mail from a friend about a friend:
        another of us joined the club.

We sit laughing around a table
and are also those three does I saw—
turning into woods, tails like white flames—
surprised on a run through melting snow
        this first pomegranate month.

I picked and ate one from the garden in
West Plainfield, barefoot in watered dirt:
its skin, juice red as leather or ribbons,
not blood, but fleshy nonetheless
        and it didn't make me stay

so I came back to this season
of hunting orange and gutter pumpkins:
just another small queen of intensive care
and telephones, hoarding these seeds
        of cold and ordinary loss.

Advice Not Given

I wanted to tell him,
the actor playing the one who returns,
briefly, in his widow's waking dream—

It's not like that. Don't avoid
eye contact, don't speak differently
from when you were alive. Nonchalance

is sharper than that sad hesitation.
When we dream them back,
they are never pale and whispering

but perfectly solid, a little younger even
than when we saw them last.
They smile, say little, sometimes take our hands.

And we always play along:
we know our lines, speak them
with proper casualness as if nothing

more momentous than opening a car
or turning on a radio were going on—
then wake full of words we didn't say.

That's how it is. I wanted to tell him,
but couldn't. I only sat backstage and listened,
hugging my knees until curtain call.

Post-Easter Syndrome

Chocolate eggs on sale
in small sealed bags.
Around that purple corner
lurks a tired joke.

The river goes on going,
the only way is down
along the empty corridor
where wasps' nests light the way.

Every day I die a little.
Every guy I leave I wonder why a little.

My nails, blue, glow
by screen light tapping.
The wait is long, the ache is easy,
the hips aren't going anywhere.

Am I going to die of this,
are the dead
trying to tell me something?
Take something for that honesty.

So where were you
when the pan was burning,
when the fox was in her den
chewing metal from her paw,

when the ghosts in the dining room
lifted their glasses:

> *having a wonderful*
> *wish you were*

What have you got to show for your tears?

More Heartbreak Survival Tips

The first song is about April and what happened.
Now the paths are white, show boot and paw for days.
New-dusted, so only the lowest spots
and roughest steps hit rich brown
smears of still-wet earth: winter
finally patting over the flow. But underneath,
turtles breathing, part of us always sea.

To write with horn bridges
falling to the resolution-seeking chorus.
To admit to any hope,
even one grounded in hopelessness,
clutching unfinished words to ribs
throughout a Holiday Season,
leaned against the sharp rungs of waiting.

The younger siblings party, long legs
folded onto matching couches,
bad white cake smeared on glossy paper plates.
Dance to the popular soundtrack
even if nobody will join in. Hips,
hands, head, heart: dance
the Willing Return, the Smiling Fool,
the Questionable Role Model.

At the car parts store, standing next to stacks of tires
with the wrong man watching through the glass:
sparks pour to the concrete ground and vanish.
You've been here before,
only it was a thousand miles way.

Moving day, other people's houses.
Heatwave in January, road of dropcloths

soft and moist, three dogs
weeping with joy at the chance to run
unchecked for hours. The neighbor boy
hands a coffeepot through the window
and it falls, glass to linoleum
shattering brightly, obvious and foreseen
and you know you'll do it again.

A movie on the VCR, lovely people
in lovely clothes being awful to each other.
The catsitter watching it from the bed
who has been crying all afternoon,
mostly into the telephone, now smiles,
mostly into the handkerchief.

Big muscular sunset through telephone wires:
sisters drive south from Lake Erie
into the vanishing countryside.
In the back seat, sacks of new used clothes,
crazy shades from decades you never saw,
pinks and purples your mothers never wore.

Stopping to buy a cabbage from a parked truckbed.
Nobody around: leave fifty cents in the coffee can
for the folded silk head, the round weight of winter.

Screenplay

Suburban kitchen, yellow gingham, etc. She shoulders the phone, one hand floating above the numbers. Looks out the window at curlered neighbor mowing lawn, black dog hurling itself against chain link.

Night. She jumps out of the car at a stoplight, dressed for a party. Laughing, she runs into the cedarbark bed of an industrial park.

Close-up of car interior. She holds out a red tulip, petals closed to a point like a fat ink marker. He smiles briefly, his face going green in the light change. He drives on.

She walks outside, rubbing the telephone side of her neck, bends to dog with a leash. Smell of an artificial lake.

Close-up of tulip in a plastic cup on a coffee table. Ashtrays, beer bottles. The flower is open now, a bowl of black furred stamens. She checks her lipstick in a pocket mirror, notices him across the crowded room alone, his arms folded, looking at nothing. She pauses, then draws a deep breath, a new mouth.

The black dog leaps at the end of its leash. She is watching the sidewalk, pulled like a puppet. Then she lets go, raising her arms above her head, turning her face to the April sky.

The tulip is flat as a plate. Smoke, swirling around it.

Map Jam

Lights dance over the mural of blue herons.
The Elbow Room's a cigar bar now. Always hectic
hummings you may not identify. Window glass
you look out most: wind clearing surfaces,
branches and wires. A wet bag lifts,
is carried, bracelets a tree.

In our minds so be it.

Black walnuts in a cardboard box.
Light comes in and out. Gratitude
to all water. Rose unfurls its thorn
stalk from the column. Lucky life
isn't one long string of pleasures.
Maple buds red, clenched. Jay cries
gather in a dent in the clouds.
Chocolate notes, chord of stars and helixes,
the spell of the sensible.

Hunkering/Frick Park

The river you can't see from here,
raccoon sipping its brink, not stepping
on shards of glass. Fastening, the
silence of parked cars after a day of rain
with lilacs browning in the back yard,
weeping the rough jewels of next year sentences,
the smell of Homewood Trail under Forbes Avenue
dank-rich as the pet fish store your father
drove you to a quarter century ago,
free stabs, sweet small carrots
overwintered in the garden left behind,
last summer's pickled peppers in a jar
still hot, still holding on.

Aliquippa Backyard, May

Mourning dove perched on Stretch's TV
antenna. Robins chat up the maple
two doors down, that sphere-crowned
cartoon-shape treeful of shadows.

Half-mackerel sky dusking, pink
jet trails. Tears this time for trays
of seedlings killed by sun and
accident, also the river dolphin

circling its pod of water at the zoo
for twenty years, a route so tight,
obsessive, they've posted a letter
by the tank from a worried visitor

and the inadequate reply. Swallows
cruise for dinner overhead. The garden's
plaster raccoon licks its red apple,
lascivious, bindweed trailing

at its feet, white slabs of good-bye cake
set out for ants and spirits.
Dove stops sighing, robins keep it down
so just now swallow-talk fills

the blue-turning air, turning—

that whir, that metal scrape
high beyond swallows, wider
flight, so far but closer and
that sound again, stick on chain-link:

nighthawks are coming through the near-
night sky to put doves, robins, swallows,
rivers, gardens, all to bed.

Vow

To praise *Marasmius*—
to remember that the hunt's
also for orange
(cayenne, turmeric, curry-colors)
and the silkstocking damp of stalk and cap,
what fingertips learn from grasping such a shape,
tiniest cocktail glass,
pin pleats of gills.

To love not just the panful, what yields
in butter, salt and heat
but what grows singly, overripe, forbidden:
sulfur knobs of *Amanita* pulling from the grass,
eggplant-hearted puffballs
lighting the dirt bike trail—
even the chanterelle the worms got to,
this yellow trumpet
laced with borings,
it has its song.

Extras

It made me look like a cross between a raccoon and a two bit whore,
someone says in line between the trailers. We are handed clothes,
shoes, escorted like dead souls at every step. We walk taller
and laughing to the hair trailer, makeup trailer. *Don't take
your curlers out. She took hers out and now she has nothing.*
They make our eyes wider, our faces bronzed
like Los Angelinos, like theirs, even the girl in headphones
leading us is beautiful, such cheekbones. No, she's not
an actress, she laughs, such grace, walking our sidewalks.
Sweat trickles under our evening wear, we smoke
too much, there is nothing else to do, if hell is other people
what afterlife is this?

They're doing Papa Was a Rolling Stone today the agent says.
We sit at empty banquet tables under watery green
chandeliers, it is before nine a.m. and we are all
in evening dress from 1973; we've learned the proper term,
not extras, *background artists.* We are in the TV movie
The Temptations. We are quiet, there will be coffee,
doughnuts soon, musicians walk in wearing powder blue
tuxedos, they look authentic but then again, it occurs to us,
so do we. Someone begins to sing, everyone stops to listen,
she is not a Supreme or a Vandella, merely one of us
but she is singing and to say this is a gift
at eight-something in the morning is as needless as the song.
She takes over the room, the day, she is better than a movie.

Grandma Called It the Magic Purse

We ran once around the house on Crabtree Lane,
dodging Grandpa's roses, Buick fenders, and when
we got back, panting like puppies
she stood holding it filled now,
same greengold purse she showed empty just before
now bulged with Milk Duds, Dum Dums, Tootsie Rolls,
and so we ate, sneakers on hot asphalt and cool lawn,
sticky with corn syrup, kinship.

Her blue guest bedroom had a bottle of lemon-scent,
goofy sixties label
but an archaic thing
to spray in air and walk through:
mist of fragrance,
summer coinage, innocence and tang,
and from this old woman's dresser top,
this wrinkled, powdered lady who drinks bourbon,
who wears diamonds and is from Iowa and hates to cook
we learn a bit of beauty,
secret smiling in a golden shower of light.

Green Glass Insulator from an Old Power Line

Fragments washed up on the beach worn smooth,
even moribund Erie did that, rubbing
sharp break to curves, easy on the hand,
shapely relic of Industrial Past I don't feel
part of. Took my museum curator mother
to convince my professor father to admire
the smoke and piles of Gary, Indiana,
father whose father laid railroads through the Midwest,
mother whose father built electrical towers,
Iowa to anywhere and back.
                              I pictured Grandpa climbing
monkey-agile up and down their laddered forms,
but he did it from a desk, pencil and slide rule.
Who wouldn't rather dream the tools of forge and press,
hot lumps of unformed metal, boots in dust,
shavings petaling the floor, glass ooze pressed
and cooling to smooth pebble, heavy goblet, bell.

Favor

Casual
       like the first dream
you were giving me a ride west.

Dressing,
         afraid of being late
I asked for help:
            picking out earrings.

     Most of my earrings yours
                admiring
     strangers laugh *She lets you wear those?*
     She's nice! And I laugh too. You are.

You picked a silver pair I love
but never saw you wear
            I've lost one now
but you were holding both
when I dreamed you at the kitchen sink
fumbling rags, pink paste,
wet hands shining for me.

Transit

Everything familiar but the light.
In nineteen years inhabiting this town
she hasn't seen this hour at any season:
cool air bodied with mist, expecting dawn,
streetlamps that changed to peach a few years back,
haloed with August humidity. The smell
hard to place at first: incense.

This hour because she isn't sure which bed
to rise from yet: behind, her first lover's,
mattress on the floor, his quilt of grandmother-
stitched polyester squares pushed to the foot,
a downtown student rental; or ahead,
in air-conditioning, her clothes in drawers,
the "big girl bed" she moved to from her crib.

The streets cathedral-still, not even a rig
gassing up on Main this hour. Possums
might walk, but it's not trash day.
One year someone saw deer browsing the square,
but that winter was hard: the family
put hay bales by the backyard's stiffened creek.
This winter's already fading, its bright snow
and hospital room grown easier to unfold,
lay smooth, repack: driving this same street home—
after they'd shut off the life support—
alone, mid-morning, through streets empty
as this one now, she'd run the family car
deliberately through a red light, smiling briefly,
thinking, I can do this today, the rules
don't count, preparing a speech, *I'm sorry officer,*

my mother's dead, I have to go home.

She has a speech prepared now too,
that she will never use,
though every morning's ride
brings her in later, rumpled and humming
until her father has brought the paper in,
is grinding coffee in the sunlit kitchen.
He's fallen in love himself, incredulous.
They watch each other shyly,
want no excuses, are unable to condemn.

It's one hour until dawn, two miles
east across town between two beds.
You can't go back. You can.

Father's Day with my Grandpa Young

He told the painter I was his son's wife.
I forget to drive us to church; make pancakes,
dressed in sweats to run crosstown, stopping

for blackberries, his son's wife's stone. The next
grave over has a nylon floral sign, DAD,
a rabbit statuette. I leave a skinny mushroom,

a fat pine cone, then run home creekside.
Unripe black walnuts bop the deck.
We talk to Ireland at five; all calm

but some concern about the cocktails.
Dad says make him a margarita. I'm wearing
Grandma's huge paisley apron.

Your dad can really mix drinks.
Grandpa repeats this several times. I run
next door for kosher salt. The apron off

though no one I know lives here now.
Miss Stacy is away so I cut across her lawn.
The dead baby grackle shining still

with flies next to Dad's large basil.
Then apron-tie, lime-slide, rim-roll,
three cubes drop and pour. Your dad

can really mix drinks. Rabbits in the graveyard
hop. Pale walnuts fall.
I forget the pretzel rod,
then I remember.

Landscape with Reservoir and Extended Family

Walks are elemental here:
        dirt path circling water,
        one side gray stones, the other
grass- and weed-covered, steep: the dog,
 a short-legged pup then, lost control
 and slid down on her belly, otter-wise.

If you like that sensation
you can roll, we show the youngest cousins.

     •

The weeds are named: Anne's lace, Becky's chicory.
 And some have games, the cousins learn:
        you can unpack the milkweed pod
        of its folded silk scarves, send them
        riding the breeze down over corn.
The field yields another: fetch the ear,
fat-kerneled bus-yellow field corn tossed—
        the dog runs again and again, sure-footed.

     •

These voices flush a heron; it flaps unhurriedly
above its double to another curve of shore.

Somewhere in that green, a sunken ship,
        unfinished clipper leaking model glue,
        launched when the dog chewed her mizzen.

So long ago, it was another dog.

.

Back at the parking-lot they collect flowers,
        children, brush off grass, check paws for mud.

  This water is man-made, young—

  but when the family drives away
        the sky, the heron, and five fishermen
        keep staring into its depth.

December 15

Heat ticking the radiator, hearts ticking
down the year. On the unmarvelous stove
red cabbage slicked with mustard oil

while at the river, geese stand in water,
flap for balance, then sail upstream
while coal sails down. Crows rest in sycamores,

night leans over everything, the glass half full.
A velvet bus goes by, half-empty,
mail comes, you fish for memories,

the river mud is full of web prints,
one white snapdragon blooms between bricks.
You can't have it all but you can have

this dusky light, the blue note chords of freight trains
full of shadows. The resolution
wide open to questions.

Torn envelopes on the cat-scratched couch.
The mass of women lead on the dance floor,
dive for the oyster, reach the pickle jar,

suck summer's watermelon rind,
hey diddle diddle, come spill your guts,
for Christmas what I want:

a star a cookbook, dog, friend, spring,
fresh start, for the world to go on spinning
with us hanging on, for the joke to be on you.

Cross-Country Flight, Bereavement Discount

Bathroom mirror before takeoff: I consider
adding painful earrings to the waif
disguise (ripped jeans, black ballcap, pearls).

Above the muzak. Learning solitude. Each exit
is equipped. Above the blue-stitched clouds,
along the sun set in horizon ribbon.

I ask for champagne,
settle for tomato juice. Cruising altitude
and almonds. You always brought
the foil packs home. The salt taste
of returning.

When you took me to the island
of the moon-goddess in winter,
swam over painted fish, I knew
it wasn't long. I held you steady
up the tiled stairs.

I will drive the cypress
to your grave, its needles
scattering on my passenger seat,
stop for pie along the Allegheny.

And eat your apples
and wear your dress,
the purple one, layered
and rustling.

What We Feel

for Eve
(February, all over again)

Shakespeare began the day I drove to you:
Macbeth, Orsino, Juliet and friends
at the Junior-Senior High in Titusville.
Still in my costume, knees and elbows bruised,
I slid and spun through dusk across I-80,
high beams on falling snow like hyperspace—
and ended in your sweatered, sleepless arms.
Now I know exactly why I came:
words, mailed gifts, can't touch you in this way.
She drove six hours, they say. Six hours,
five years—it's nothing. Is the hardest part
ahead? Behind you now? Drive carefully.

Not sure how much my own loss brought me here,
I still feel privileged to know a bit
of what it's like to be you at this time.
That's why I draw you into giddy laughter,
help you eat cookies (always, there are cookies),
show you my latest thrift store finds. You have
to have the handkerchief with rows of hearts.
Next day, we float above our dressed-up selves.
Your mother's friend speaks of her beauty. I
look over at your face, a lovely mask.
Today the sky's a blank, familiar blue.
I must drive into it again, leave you

with everything, with cookies growing stale.
The weight of this sad time we must obey.
The high school kids aren't ready for these words.
We that are young, but not as young as that,
can speak them now, speak what we feel, or try.

Walking Around Meadville, PA

I am sick of being an actress.
I spend hours in chalky upstairs rooms
shivering at card tables with sour telephones,
useless, losing color, like a jet trail
    dissolving in washed empty dusk.
A gazebo in snow makes me ache for five months gone.

The only thing I want is to see no more photographs of myself,
no sawhorses, no business cards, no gel frames, no hats.
The only thing I want is to sit in a room lined with books
and hear bread rise.
The only thing I want is a door bell,
mud on my shoes, junk mail, a week of nothing.
I am sick of my eyelids and my jaw, my abdominal muscles,
my knees, my voice that keeps changing its tone.

I don't want to go on traveling,
sorting cassettes in shoeboxes,
applying lipstick in the rearview,
stepping through slush in vinyl dress shoes,
shaking the hands of women with glasses hung on chains.

I don't want so much romance,
iambics in the laundromat,
prop bottles filled at enamel high school fountains,
acoustics testing in unlit dusty halls,
civic lunches and poster board and taffeta.

That's why I walk.
At night the small town twists in its sleep.
There are shadows of leaves ironed on the sidewalk,
there are killdeer crying in the baseball diamond.
There are thin bruised dogs cowering on the bridge,

there are bracelets of ice on the pier.
There are four Amish boys following their shoes.

I walk along with my empty hands in used gloves,
my throat, my hunger, remembering,
    self-conscious tears pressed through a blink.
I walk past rectangles of lawn, each one different;
past windows full of lamps, mirrors, and backs;
looking straight into each box of walls and heat,
my nameless boots scraping the blurred curb,
homesick for nowhere I've been yet.

Nothing but This

your past spelled out in shoes
    a biscuit tin of torn receipts
        thieves camped in a circle outside the village
            frying up scraps of leather

that glitter on the street is mica

it's a game you wake to yourself
alone in the night when it matters
    hands warmed on a dog's belly
    walking out below an onion moon
    trees dripping like stone fountains

you collect phrases like baseball cards
each slick foil package wraps one
    they slide to the floor like supermarket inserts
    each time you open hands, a folded towel
        a box of teabags from the cupboard
        the rolled mail from its coffin.

The Black Dog

comes to your whistle after roaming
the corners of Walt and Emily,
curb and lamppost,
rhythm mud and meter hydrant.
Panting and yellow-eyed, he's like a cat
on steroids, rides the subway at night
gets off at the stop just before home
so he can trot the last five blocks alone,
passes the half-shut gate of the courtyard
with the lemons, across from a bank
of pay phones one of which is ringing
he doesn't pick it up but presses through
the gate and finds a fallen still-firm lemon,
carries it past trash piles, sleeping pigeons,
homeless pushing shopping carts, and home to you.
The lemon gentle in his teeth, there is not one
bruise on it, it smells like heaven, he smells
like wet dog, and you take it.